Angels Over Elsinore

ALSO BY CLIVE JAMES

CLIVE JAMES

Angels Over Elsinore

COLLECTED VERSE 2003–2008

PICADOR

First published 2008 by Picador
an imprint of Pan Macmillan Ltd
Pan Macmillan, 20 New Wharf Road, London N1 9RR
Basingstoke and Oxford
Associated companies throughout the world
www.panmacmillan.com

ISBN 978-0-330-45740-8

A CIP catalogue record for this book is available from
the British Library.

Printed in the UK by CPI Mackays, Chatham ME5 8TD

To Stephen Edgar

Acknowledgements

My thanks are due to the editors of the *Australian*, the *Australian Literary Review*, the *Monthly*, *Meanjin*, the *Australian Book Review*, the *Times Literary Supplement*, the *Spectator*, the *Guardian*, the *London Review of Books*, the *Liberal*, *Standpoint*, the *New York Times*, *Poetry (Chicago)* and the *New Yorker*. 'Les Saw It First' made its debut in the Festschrift for Les Murray, *Letters to Les*, published by the Mildura Festival. I would also like to thank the various editors of the annual anthologies *The Best Australian Poems* and *The Best Australian Poetry* for their generous harbouring of a carpetbagger. The poem 'Ramifications of Pure Beauty' first appeared in *The Book of My Enemy*, but it needed revision because of factual errors, so I have given it another run. I am well aware that the title of 'Status Quo Vadis' is bad Latin. But it is an exact transcription of a line in the film *Strictly Ballroom*, and therefore has classic status of a kind. Finally, my thanks to Don Paterson for his detailed comments and for choosing the order.

Contents

Windows Is Shutting Down

Windows is shutting down, and grammar are
On their last leg. So what am we to do?
A letter of complaint go just so far,
Proving the only one in step are you.

Better, perhaps, to simply let it goes.
A sentence have to be screwed pretty bad
Before they gets to where you doesnt knows
The meaning what it must of meant to had.

The meteor have hit. Extinction spread,
But evolution do not stop for that.
A mutant languages rise from the dead
And all them rules is suddenly old hat.

Too bad for we, us what has had so long
The best seat from the only game in town.
But there it am, and whom can say its wrong?
Those are the break. Windows is shutting down.

Angels Over Elsinore

How many angels knew who Hamlet was
When they were summoned by Horatio?
They probably showed up only because
The roster said it was their turn to go.

Another day, another Dane. Too bad,
But while they sang their well-rehearsed lament
They noticed his good looks. Too soon, too sad,
This welcome home for what seemed heaven sent.

Imagine having been with him down there!
But here I dream, for angels do not yearn.
They take up their positions in the air
Free from the passions of the earth they spurn.

Even their singing is done less from joy
Than duty. But was this the usual thing?
Surely they gazed on that recumbent boy,
Clearly cut out one day to be a king,

And sang him to his early rest above
With soaring pride that they should form the choir
Whose voices echoed all the cries of love,
Which, even when divine, implies desire?

But soft: an ideal world does not exist.
Hamlet went nowhere after he was dead.
No angel sighed where lovers never kissed,
And there was nothing in what his friend said.

Hamlet himself knew just what to expect:
Steady reduction of his body mass
Until the day, his very coffin wrecked,
Some clown picked up his skull and said, 'Alas.'

No, there would be no music from on high.
No feather from a wing would fall, not one.
Forget it all, even the empty sky –
What's gone is gone, sweet prince. What's done is done.

Exit Don Giovanni

Somewhere below his pride, the Don's bad dreams
Fashioned the statue that would take him down.
Deep underground, the tears were there in streams.
The man who had the only game in town,

In Spain, in Europe, when it came to love,
Sensed that there had to be a reckoning.
The boundaries he claimed to soar above
Meant nothing to him except everything.

Why the defiant stance, if not from shame?
And why deny that truth, if not from fear?
The bodice-ripper made his famous name
By staying buttoned up. His whole career

Came back to haunt him in a stony glance.
Transfixed, he followed where the statue led.
Below, tips of hot tongues began to dance.
Further below, it was a sea of red.

There was a jetty. Next to it, a raft
Held every name on Leporello's list,
Even from just last week. The statue laughed
And left. The women, modelled out of mist,

Were images, as they had always been
To him, but strong enough to ply the sweeps.
They would not meet his eye, having foreseen
What waited for him on the burning deeps.

A long way out, they paused, and one by one
They disappeared, each hinting with a smile,
But not to him, their work had been well done.
He was alone. To cry was not his style,

But then he reached down through the surface fire
Into the water. Almost with relief
He learned at last the flames of his desire
Had floated on the ocean of his grief.

Had he known sooner, what would that have meant?
Less to regret, and little to admit?
The raft burned: final stage of his descent.
Hell was on Earth. Now he was out of it.

My Father Before Me

Sai Wan War Cemetery, Hong Kong

At noon, no shadow. I am on my knees
Once more before your number and your name.
The usual heat, the usual fretful bees
Fitfully busy as last time I came.

Here you have lain since 1945,
When you, at half the age that I am now,
Were taken from the world of the alive,
Were taken out of time. You should see how

This hillside, since I visited it first,
Has stayed the same. Nothing has happened here.
They trim the sloping lawn and slake its thirst.
Regular wreaths may fade and reappear,

But these are details. High on either side
Waves of apartment blocks roll in so far
And no further, forbidden to collide
By laws that keep the green field where you are,

Along with all these others, sacrosanct.
For once the future is denied fresh ground.
For that much if no more, let God be thanked.
You can't see me or even hear the sound

Of my voice, though it comes out like the cry
You heard from me before you sailed away.
Your wife, my mother, took her turn to die
Not long ago. I don't know what to say –

Except those many years she longed for you
Are over now at last, and now she wears
The same robes of forgetfulness you do.
When the dreams cease, so do the nightmares.

I know you would be angry if I said
I, too, crave peace. Besides, it's not quite so.
Despair will ebb when I leave you for dead
Once more. Once more, as I get up to go,

I look up to the sky, down to the sea,
And hope to see them, while I still draw breath,
The way you saw your photograph of me
The very day you flew to meet your death.

Back at the gate, I turn to face the hill,
Your headstone lost again among the rest.
I have no time to waste, much less to kill.
My life is yours; my curse, to be so blessed.

A Gyre from Brother Jack

The canvas, called *A Morning Long Ago*,
Hangs now in Dublin's National Gallery
Of Ireland, and for capturing the flow
Of life, its radiant circularity,
Yeats painter leaves Yeats poet beaten flat.
I hear you saying, 'How can he say that?'

But look. Here is the foyer of a grand
Theatre. It is always interval.
On the upper level, brilliant people stand.
What they have seen inside invests them all
With liquid light, and some of them descend
The sweet, slow, curving, anti-clockwise bend

Of staircase and go out into that park
Where yet another spectacle has formed:
A lake made bright by the oncoming dark.
And at the left of that, white wings have stormed
Upward towards where this rondeau begins.
Birds? Angels? Avatars? Forgiven sins?

He doesn't say: the aspect I like best.
William had theories. Jack has just the thrill.
We see a little but we miss the rest,
And what we keep to ponder, time will kill.
The lives we might have led had we but known
Check out at dawn and take off on their own

Even as we arrive. Sad, it might seem,
When talked about: but shown, it shines like day.
The only realistic general scheme
Of the divine is in this rich display –
Proof that the evanescent present tense
Is made eternal by our transience.

Woman Resting

Sometimes the merely gifted give us proof
Born artists have a democratic eye
That genius gets above, to stand aloof,
Scorning to seize on all that happens by

And give it the full treatment. Look at her,
Mancini's woman, as she rests her head
In white impasto linen. Cats would purr
To think of lying curled up on that bed

Warmed by her Monica Bellucci skin.
Her mouth, like Vitti's in *La Notte*, breathes
A sulky need for more of the same sin
That knocked her sideways. Silently, she seethes.

She's perfect, and he's well up to the task
Of illustrating her full bloom of youth.
Why isn't she immortal, then? you ask.
Look at her bedside table for the truth.

Carafe, decanter, bottle, beaker, all
Are brushed in with the same besotted touch:
Not just as clutter which, were it to fall,
Would break and be swept up. He cares too much

About the world around her. While she dreams,
The room dreams too, as if it too were spent
From pleasure. In the end, nothing redeems
This failure to make her the main event.

Manet's Olympia is no great shakes
For beauty beside this one, but transcends
Her setting with exactly what it takes:
The fire that starts where general interest ends.

Out for the count, Miss Italy sleeps on,
So lovely that we check the artist's name,
Vow to remember it, and then are gone,
Forgetting one who never found his fame

Because his unrestricted sympathy
Homogenised existence. Art must choose
What truly merits perpetuity
From everything that we are bound to lose.

Even a master's landscape, though devoid
Of people, has a human soul in view:
His own. A focused vision is employed
To say: behold what I alone can do.

Picking the mortal to immortalise,
The great paint objects only to abet
Their concentration on what lives and dies.
Faced with a woman that they can't forget

They make sure we can't either. Should she rest,
Her daylight hours still dominate the room.
We see her waking up and getting dressed.
Her silence hits us like the crack of doom.

But this girl, drowned in décor, disappears
From memory, which doesn't care to keep
A pretty picture long, so save your tears.
I shouldn't try to wake her. Let her sleep,

And let Mancini, suave but second rate,
Sleep with her, as in fact he might have done –
Some recompense for his eventual fate
Of scarcely mattering to anyone.

Sunday Morning Walk

Frost on the green.
The ducks cold-footing it across the grass
Beside the college moat

Meet a clutch of matrons
In freeze-dried Barbours
Walking their collies
Freshly brushed by Gainsborough.

Buoyed by the world's supply
Of rosemary sprigs
Packed under glass,

The moorcock emerging from the reeds
Does a hesitation step
As though dancing to Piazzolla.
Cool shoes, if I may say so.

In front of the boat-houses
The rowers rigging fulcrums to the shells
Bite off their gloves
To push in pins,

And the metal shines
Just short of a glitter
Because the light, though Croesus-rich,
Is kiss-soft.

Under the bridge, the iron ribs
Form a pigeon loft,
A pit-lane of sports saloons
Testing their engines.

The final year
Of the finishing school for swans
Passes in review,
Watched by the cob, his nibs,

Who at Bayreuth once
Had a glide-on role
In *Lohengrin*,
But this is better.

Winter regatta,
Unspoiled by even
Yesterday's litter
Spilling from the bins,

Is it any wonder
That I never left you?
Remember this day,
It's already melting.

Natural Selection

The gradual but inexorable magic
That turned the dinosaurs into the birds
Had no overt, only a hidden, logic.
To start the squadrons climbing from the herds
No wand was ever waved, but afterwards
Those who believed there must have been a wizard
Said the whole show looked too well-planned for hazard.

And so it does, in retrospect. Such clever
Transitions, intricate beyond belief!
The little lobsters, in their mating fever,
Assaulted from the sea, stormed up the cliff,
And swept inland as scorpions. But if
Some weapons freak equipped their tails for murder
He must have thought sheer anguish all in order.

Source of all good and hence of evil, pleasure
And hence of pain, he is, or else they are,
Without a moral sense that we can measure,
And thus without a mind. Better by far
To stand in awe of blind chance than to fear
A conscious mechanism of mutation
Bringing its fine intentions to fruition

Without a qualm about collateral horror.
The peacock and the tapeworm both make sense.
Nobody calls the ugly one an error.
But when a child is born to pain intense
Enough to drive its family all at once
To weep blood, an intelligent designer
Looks like a torture garden's beaming owner.

No, give it up. The world demands our wonder
Solely because no feeling brain conceived
The thumb that holds the bamboo for the panda.
Creation, if the thing's to be believed –
And only through belief can life be loved –
Must do without that helping hand from Heaven.
Forget it, lest it never be forgiven.

Under the Jacarandas

Under the jacarandas
The pigeons and the gulls
Pick at the fallen purple
That inundates the grass
For two weeks in October.

Although the splash of colour
Should seem absurdly lush,
Soon you get used to it.
You think life is like that,
But a clock is ticking.

The pigeons and the gulls
Don't even know how good
They look, set off like this.
They get it while it's there.
Keep watching and you'll learn.

The Victor Hugo Clematis

In our garden, the Victor Hugo clematis
Grows among masses of small pink roses
Prettier than it is, but not as stately.
There's a royal lustre to its purple petals:
Long splinters of amethyst
Arranged like the ribs of a Catherine wheel
In a disc that is almost all space,
And the edge of every petal
Is curved like the volutes in any of the four
Propellers of the *Normandie*,
Those museum-forecourt-filling pieces of sculpture
(37 tons each of cast manganese bronze)
That transmitted the electric
Power to the water,
Giving the ship her all-conquering speed,
Not to mention her teeth-rattling vibration
Even in First Class –
The cost of elegance, as the Victor Hugo clematis
Costs me my equilibrium,
Until I wonder: don't I mean the narrow-bladed
More-wood-than-metal airscrew
Of a WWI Armée de l'Air bomber?
Say a Breguet 14, faster than a Fokker D VII?
Perhaps that would be better:
I grow uncertain, I have to look things up,
And stuff that I thought I knew for sure
Turns out to be wrong.

Inelegantly reclining in my liner chair
As the evening sunlight finally fades,
I watch the flowers, that were never really my thing,
Glowing their last and blacking out closer
And closer to me
(When the dancing finished in the Grand Salon
At one o'clock in the morning
They brought back and unrolled the half-ton weight
Of the world's biggest ocean-going carpet
To cover the parquetry floor
Copied from the throne-room in Versailles)
While the great poet's record-breaker of a funeral
Still stretches half way across Paris –
Well, it does in my mind –
And the rockets and flares go up to look for Gothas –
I can see the colours burst and fall, going dry
Like the baby dribble of cherubim
On a black velvet bib –
And the pinwheel flower, even in silhouette,
Drills a sibilant echo of Cocteau's voice through my brain's ruins:
The Victor Hugo clematis is a madman that thinks
It is Victor Hugo.

Mystery of the Silver Chair

As if God's glory, with just one sun-ray,
Could not burn craters in a chromosome,
We call it kindly when it works our way,
And, some of us with tact, some with display,
Arrange the house to make it feel at home.

With votive tokens we propitiate
Almighty God. Just to be neat and clean –
Running the water hot to rinse the plate,
Chipping the rust-flakes from the garden gate –
These things are silent prayers, meant to be seen.

Strange, though, when parents with a stricken child
Still cleanse the temple, purify themselves.
They were betrayed, but how do they run wild?
With J-cloth and a blob of Fairy Mild
They wipe the white gloss of the kitchen shelves.

They, least of all, are likely to let go
Completely, like the slovens down the street:
The ones who could conceal a buffalo
In their front lawn and you would never know,
Yet somehow they keep their Creator sweet.

Unjust, unjust: but only if He's there.
The girl with palsy looks you in the eye,
Seeming to say there is no God to care.
Her gleaming wheel-chair says He's everywhere,
Or why would the unwell try not to die?

And why would those who love them give the best
Years of their lives to doing the right thing?
Why go on passing a perpetual test
With no real hope and with so little rest?
Why make from suffering an offering?

Why dust the carpet, wash the car, dress well?
If God were mocked by those who might do that
With ample cause, having been given Hell
To live with, we could very quickly tell –
Somebody would forget to feed the cat.

Sometimes they do. Sometimes the spirit kneels.
But when those with the least take pride the most,
We need to bend our thoughts to how it feels.
Shamed by those scintillating silver wheels,
We see the lightning of the Holy Ghost.

The Genesis Wafers

Genesis carried wafers in her hold
To catch the particles sent from the sun.
Diamond, sapphire, gold
Were those fine webs, as if by spiders spun
Beside whom specks of dust would weigh a ton.

A million miles from Earth, in the deep cold,
The particles collected in the skeins.
Diamond, sapphire, gold,
They flowered like tiny salt pans in the rains –
Fresh tablecloths distressed with coffee stains.

Back in the lab, the altered wafers told
A story of how poetry is born:
Diamond, sapphire, gold
Serenities invaded by stuff torn
From the incandescent storm that powers the dawn.

Museum of the Unmoving Image

The objects on display might seem to lack
Significance, unless you know the words.
The final straw that broke the camel's back,
The solitary stone that killed two birds.

Does this stuff really merit a glass case?
A tatty mattress and a shrivelled pea,
A shadow that somebody tried to chase,
A rusty pin that somehow earned a fee?

That gilded lily might have looked quite good
Without the dust that you won't see me for.
But where's the thrill in one piece of touched wood?
I think we've seen that uncut ice before.

A strained-at gnat, how interesting is that?
The bat from hell looks pitifully tame,
As do the pickled tongue got by the cat,
The ashes of the moth drawn to the flame.

Spilled milk, rough diamond, gift horse, gathered moss,
Dead duck, gone goose, bad apple, busted flush –
They're all lined up as if we gave a toss.
Try not to kill each other in the crush.

They've got an annexe for the big events:
Burned boats and bridges, castles in the air,
Clouds for your head to be in, rows of tents
For being camp as. Do we have to care?

What does this junk add up to? Look and learn,
The headphones say. They say our language grew
Out of this bric-a-brac. Here we return
To when the world around us shone brand new,

Lending its lustre to what people said;
Their speech was vivid with specific things.
It cries out to be brought back from the dead.
See what it was, and hear what it still sings.

Statement from the Secretary of Defense

This one we didn't know we didn't know:
At least, I didn't. You, you might have known
You didn't know. Let's say that might be so.
You knew, with wisdom granted you alone,

You didn't know. You say, but don't say how,
You knew we didn't know about abuse,
By us, in gaols of theirs that we run now.
Well, now we all know. I make no excuse:

In fact it's far worse than you think. You thought
You knew how bad it was? If you could see
The photos in this classified report
You'd know you knew, as usual, less than me.

You want to see a stress position? Look
At how I crouch to meet the President
And tell him this has not gone by the book.
How do I know he won't know what I meant?

I just know what he'll say, with hanging head:
'They don't know what pain is, these foreign folks.
Pain is to know you don't know what gets said
Behind your back, except you know the jokes.'

I feel for that man in his time of trial.
He simply didn't know, but now he knows
He didn't, and it hurts. Yet he can smile.
Remember how that Arab saying goes –

The blow that doesn't break you makes you strong?
They'll thank us when they get up off the mat.
They didn't know we knew what they knew. Wrong.
Even our women can do stuff like that.

Fair-weather friends who called our cause so good
Not even we could screw it, but now say
We've managed the impossible – I've stood
All I can stand of petty spite today,

So leave no room for doubt: now that we know
We might have known we didn't know, let's keep
Our heads. Give history time, and time will show
How flags wash clean, and eagles cease to weep.

The Australian Suicide Bomber's Heavenly Reward

Here I am, complaining as usual to Nicole Kidman
('Sometimes I think that to you I'm just a sex object')
While I watch Elle McPherson model her new range
Of minimalist lingerie.
Elle does it the way I told her,
Dancing slowly to theme music from *The Sirens*
As she puts the stuff on instead of taking it off.
Meanwhile, Naomi Watts is fluffing up the spare bed
For her re-run of that scene in *Mulholland Drive*
Where she gets it on with the brunette with the weird name.
In keeping with the requirements of ethnic origin
Naomi's partner here will be Portia de Rossi,
Who seems admirably hot for the whole idea.
On every level surface there are perfumed candles
And wind chimes tinkle on the moonlit terrace:
Kylie and Dannii are doing a great job.
(They fight a lot, but when I warn them they might miss
Their turn, they come to heel.)
Do you know, I was scared I might never make it?
All suited up in my dynamite new waistcoat,
I was listening to our spiritual leader –
Radiant his beard, elegant his uplifted finger –
As he enthrallingly outlined, not for the first time,
The blessings that awaited us upon the successful completion
Of our mission to obliterate the infidel.
He should never have said he was sorry
He wasn't going with us.
Somehow I found myself pushing the button early.
I remember his look of surprise
In the flash of light before everything went sideways,

And I thought I might have incurred Allah's displeasure.
But Allah, the Greatest, truly as great as they say –
Great in his glory, glorious in his greatness, you name it –
Was actually waiting for me at the front door of this place
With a few words of his own. 'You did the right thing.
Those were exactly the people to lower the boom on.
Did they really think that I, of all deities,
Was ever going to be saddled with all that shit?
I mean, *please*. Hello? Have we met?'
And so I was escorted by the Hockeyroos –
Who had kindly decided to dress for beach volleyball –
Into the antechamber where Cate Blanchett was waiting
In a white bias-cut evening gown and bare feet.
High maintenance, or what?
No wonder I was feeling a bit wrecked.
'You look,' she said, 'as if you could use a bath.'
She ran it for me, whisking the foam with her fingertips
While adding petals of hydrangeas and nasturtiums.
Down at her end, she opened a packet of Jaffas
And dropped them in, like blood into a cloud.

Diamond Pens of the Bus Vandals

Where do bus vandals get their diamond pens
That fill each upstairs window with a cloud
Of shuffled etchings? Patience does them proud.
Think of Spinoza when he ground a lens.

A fog in London used to be outside
The bus, which had to crawl until it cleared.
Now it's as if the world had disappeared
In shining smoke however far you ride.

You could call this a breakthrough, of a sort.
These storms of brilliance, light as the new dark,
Disturb and question like a pickled shark:
Conceptual art free from the bonds of thought,

Raw talent rampant. New York subway cars
Once left poor Jackson Pollock looking tame.
Some of the doodlers sprayed their way to fame:
A dazzled Norman Mailer called them stars.

And wasn't Michelangelo, deep down,
Compelled to sling paint by an empty space,
Some ceiling he could thoroughly deface?
The same for Raphael. When those boys hit town

Few of its walls were safe. One cave in France
Has borne for almost forty thousand years
Pictures of bison and small men with spears –
Blank surfaces have never stood a chance

Against the human impulse to express
The self. All those initials on the glass
Remind you, as you clutch your Freedom Pass,
It's a long journey from the wilderness.

The Zero Pilot

On the *Hiryu*, Hajime Toyoshima
Starred in the group photos like Andy Hardy,
He was so small and cute.
His face, as friendly as his first name
(In Japanese you say 'Hajime' at first meeting),
Could have been chirping, 'Hey, why don't we
Put the show on right here in the barn?'
After Pearl Harbor he was one of the great ship's heroes
And the attack on Darwin promised him yet more glory,
But his engine conked out over Melville Island
From one lousy rifle bullet in the oil system.
Caught by natives, he should have done it then,
If not beforehand when the prop stopped turning.
Instead of hitting the silk
He could have nosed over and dived into the ground
But he didn't. When the natives closed in
He could have shot himself with his .32
But he didn't do that either.
Under interrogation he was offered chocolate
Which he ate instead of turning down.
What was he thinking of?
He didn't get it done
Until a full two and half years later –
After the Cowra breakout, which he helped
To lead, madly blowing a stolen bugle,
Psyched up to guide his party of frantic runners
All the way to Japan. Upon recapture
He finally did it with a carving knife,
Sawing at his own throat as if to cancel
That sweet, rich taste of surrender,

The swallowed chocolate. His ruined Zero
Is on display in Darwin. The empty bulkhead
Is torn like silver paper where the engine roared
That once propelled him through the startled sky
At a rate of roll unknown to Kittyhawks.
Paint, cables, webbing, instruments and guns:
Much else is also missing,
But the real absence is his,
And always was.
'Hajime' is short for
'Our acquaintanceship begins:
Until now, we did not know each other.
From this day forth, we will.'
Well, could be,
Though it mightn't be quite that easy.
Buried at Cowra,
He probably never knew
That the *Hiryu* went down at Midway,
Where the last of his friends died fighting –
Still missing the cheery voice
Of their mascot, named always to say hello,
Who never said goodbye.

Iron Horse

The Sioux, believing ponies should be pintos,
Painted the ones that weren't.
When they saw the Iron Horse
They must have wondered why the palefaces
Left its black coat unmarked.
Bruno Schulz said an artist must mature
But only into childhood.
He called our first perceptions
The iron capital of the adult brain.
I would like to think my latest marquetry
Was underpinned by Debussy's *Images*
Or the chain of micro-essays
In Adorno's *Minima moralia*,
But a more likely progenitor
Entered my head right here in Sydney:
The first aesthetic thrill that I remember.
In a Strand Arcade display case
A tiny but fine-detailed model train
Ran endlessly around a plaster landscape.
On tip-toe, looking through the panorama
Rather than down on it, I formed or fed
Lasting ideals of mimesis, precision
And the consonance of closely fitted parts
Combined into a work that had coherence
Beyond its inseparable workings.
Later, at the flicks, when the Iron Horse
Was attacked by yelping braves,
I heard their hoof-beats on a marble floor,
And later still, having read about steam power
In my *Modern Marvels Encyclopaedia*,

When I realised the little train
Had been pulled by an illusionary loco –
Directly turned by an electric motor,
The wheels propelled the rods and not vice versa –
My seeing through the trick only increased
The recollection of intensity,
Immensity compressed into a bubble,
The macrosphere in miniature.
But mere shrinkage didn't work the magic:
There had to be that complicated movement
Of intricate articulation
As in an aero-engine like the Merlin
Or the H-form Napier Sabre.
In the Hermitage, a Fabergé toy train
Was not so precious, didn't even go,
Was hopelessly disfigured by its jewels.
It left me with pursed lips and shaking head,
Surprised they even bothered
And full of pity for the royal children
Deceived by their bonanza every Christmas –
A wampum headband set with amethysts,
A solid silver tomahawk –
Into equating workmanship with wealth.
Full of boutiques that try to do the same,
The Strand Arcade is still there,
Commendably preserved if over-polished,
But the train is gone for good –
Except where, in my mind,
Forever turning back and yet forever
Continuing its *tour d'horizon*
Of a world threatened by a race of giants,
It snickers behind the glass
I stained with the acid of my fingertips.

Grace Cossington Smith's Harbour Bridge

Grace Cossington Smith, Grace Cossington Smith,
Your name is yet one to be conjuring with.
You painted the Bridge well before it was finished
And still the excitement remains undiminished,
Your patchwork of pigments enhancing its myth.

Grace Cossington Smith, Grace Cossington Smith,
Your skill was the essence, the fulcrum and pith
Of all that we love about classical art
Embracing the modern and making it part
Of the total adventure that starts in the heart.

Crace Cossington Smith, Grace Cossington Smith,
Your moniker honours your kin and your kith.
The studies you made of the Bridge uncompleted
Add up to a triumph that can't be repeated:
The lattice-work elements reach for each other
Like Damon and Pythias, brother to brother,
Imprinting the sky with the future before it
Was certain, and you were the one who foresaw it.
The polychrome grains of our grey megalith –
You put them together, Grace Cossington Smith.

Belated Homage to Derek Walcott

You made me think last night. Your lines about
How people on those islands you evoke
As easily as blowing smoke
Could not look down from high ground to the sea,
Or even see a cargo ship, without
Fear of the worst, reminded me –
Reminded me I still need the reminder –
That my own ships and oceans linked a kinder
Imperium. Though free for generations
The crime's descendants are not free of that –
The open water is for drowning in.
Embarked now for the erstwhile ruling nations,
The migrant's back still hears the spitting cat.
He looks up through the grille at the least grin
Of condescension. Railway station porters
With one impatient word rape teenage daughters –
Terror invades perception when it gives
That tinge of death to where your verse most lives,
In the lost luxuriance
Of how you, growing up, were made to feel
By history that your childhood was unreal
Because the actual so usurped romance
That even the sweet white of breaking waves –
Their stately bridal veils of spray –
Looked startling as the bones of broken slaves:
Unsleeping infrastructure of the trance
The tourist brochures lovingly display,
Taking your time out of their time away.

You made me think last night, but not today.
Today I found out that a girl I know
Was bailed up by two little boys in hoods
Who claimed their hidden knives were not for show.
She made a weapon of her front-door key.
They took off. No doubt short of worldly goods
Through no fault of their own, they make me long
To see them kicked and whipped. Don't get me wrong:
Where she lives, there are whites the same age worse.
But let's not kid ourselves. Race is a curse,
And at a time like this it curses me.
To put it bluntly, I don't think at all.
Terror invades perception:
Reaction, ruled by what we first recall,
Enrols an ethnic type without exception
Among the threats to life, as it must do
Even for you. Tell me that isn't so.
Hand on your heart and say it isn't true.

You made me think last night. How can I know
Your deepest wish is not for me to go
To Hell? Should I pretend I understand
What it feels like, before the burning sand
And scalding water teach me how to die
Day in, day out, under that pretty sky?
Before I, too, can hear in the surf's roar
The landlady's slammed door,
Can see the lynch mob strutting with the gulls
Gathered among the hulls
Of yachts whose owners don't just patronise
A raw colonial, but spurn my hand
And still would if it held the Nobel Prize –
Proof of my right to land

Having sailed so far, and, stranger yet, survived
A setting out from which so few arrived,
And fewer still thrived, on the further shore?
I know: I should have thought of this before.

When We Were Kids

When we were kids we fought in the mock battle
With Ned Kelly cap guns and we opened the cold bottle
Of Shelley's lemonade with a Scout belt buckle.
We cracked the passion fruit and sipped the honeysuckle.

When we were kids we lit the Thundercracker
Under the fruit tin and we sucked the all day sucker.
We opened the shoe box to watch the silk-worms spinning
Cocoons of cirrus with oriental cunning.

When we were kids we were sun-burned to a frazzle.
The beach was a griddle, you could hear us spit and sizzle.
We slept face down when our backs came out in blisters.
Teachers were famous for throwing blackboard dusters.

When we were kids we dive-bombed from the tower.
We floated in the inner tube, we bowled the rubber tyre.
From torn balloons we blew the cherry bubble.
Blowing up Frenchies could get you into trouble.

When we were kids we played at cock-a-lorum.
Gutter to gutter the boys ran harum-scarum.
The girls ran slower and their arms and legs looked funny.
You weren't supposed to drink your school milk in the dunny.

When we were kids the licorice came in cables.
We traded Hubba-Bubba bubblegum for marbles.
A new connie-agate was a flower trapped in crystal
Worth just one go with a genuine air pistol.

When we were kids we threw the cigarette cards
Against the wall and we lined the Grenadier Guards
Up on the carpet and you couldn't touch the trifle
Your Aunt Marge made to go in the church raffle.

When we were kids we hunted the cicada.
The pet cockatoo bit like a barracuda.
We were secret agents and fluent in pig Latin.
Gutsing on mulberries made our lips shine like black satin.

When we were kids we caught the Christmas beetle.
Its brittle wings were gold-green like the wattle.
Our mothers made bouquets from frangipani.
Hard to pronounce, a pink musk-stick cost a penny.

When we were kids we climbed peppercorns and willows.
We startled the stingrays when we waded in the shallows.
We mined the sand dunes in search of buried treasure,
And all this news pleased our parents beyond measure.

When we were kids the pus would wet the needle
When you dug out splinters and a piss was called a piddle.
The scabs on your knees would itch when they were ready
To be picked off your self-renewing body.

When we were kids a year would last forever.
Then we grew up and were told it was all over.
Now we are old and the memories returning
Are like the last stars that fade before the morning.

Only Divine

Always the Gods learned more from humankind
Than vice versa. So it was bound to be:
It takes a troubled heart to make a mind.
Stuck with their beautiful stupidity,

The Gods were peeved to find themselves outclassed
Even in pleasure, which was their best thing.
Sky-walking Zeus, the Bright One, was aghast
To find that men could laugh and weep and sing

For love, instead of merely chasing tail
The way he did when he came down to earth:
Driving his lightning bolt in like a nail,
Shouting the place down with unsubtle mirth.

Sometimes he stole earth-men's identities.
His acrobatics in a borrowed face
Drew some applause for their raw power to please
But none at all for foreplay, tact or grace.

By Jove! By Jupiter! He heard the names
Men gave him change. The world grew less impressed
Than he was with his simple fun and games,
The gold medallions on his hairy chest.

Back in the clouds, he brooded for as long
As Gods can. If he couldn't have the tears
Of mortals, he could copy a love song.
To learn one took him several hundred years,

But time, like sorrow, doesn't count up there.
He got quite good at it, and now he sings
Sinatra standards that sound pretty fair
Against a backing track complete with strings.

Virgin Minerva, born out of his brain
To stave off Vulcan with a single slap,
Borrowed more fetching versions of disdain
Better designed to milk the thunderclap

Of lust. Her heavenly suitors pay for shoes
She might wear only once, or not at all.
Pretending they know how it feels to lose,
Prospective lovers, outside in the hall,

Compare TAG Heuer watches while they scuff
Their Gucci loafers on the marble floor.
In love, real men have taught them, things get rough:
A show of grief might get you through her door.

Inside, she lies back on her Zsa-Zsa pink
Chaise-longue while Aphrodite dishes dirt.
Feigning to taste the whisky sours they drink,
They smile as if a memory could hurt.

Does Atlas need those Terminator shades?
Poseidon's wet-suit, what good does it do?
Is gold-crowned Phoebe on her roller blades
Really as cute as when the world was new?

And here comes Hera in her Britney kit,
And there goes Hermes on his superbike.
The stuff they have! You wouldn't credit it,
And all top of the range. What are they *like*?

Like us, without the creativity
Stirred by the guilt that hangs around our necks.
Their only care the void of their carefree
Millennia of unprotected sex,

Uncomprehendingly they quote our books.
Their gull-wing sports cars and their Gulfstream jets,
The bling-bling wasted on their perfect looks –
It's all ours. Gleaming as their long sun sets,

The Gods are gaudy tatters of a plan
Hatched by our ancestors to render fate
More bearable. They end as they began,
Belittled in our thoughts that made them great.

Lock Me Away

In the NHS psychiatric test
For classifying the mentally ill
You have to spell 'world' backwards.
Since I heard this, I can't stop doing it.
The first time I tried pronouncing the results
I got a sudden flaring picture
Of Danny La Rue in short pants
With his mouth full of marshmallows.
He was giving his initial and surname
To a new schoolteacher.
Now every time I read the *Guardian*
I find its columns populated
By a thousand mumbling drag queens.
Why, though, do I never think
Of a French film composer
(Georges Delerue, pupil of
Darius Milhaud, composed the waltz
In *Hiroshima, Mon Amour*)
Identifying himself to a policeman
After being beaten up?
But can I truly say I never think of it
After I've just thought of it?
Maybe I'm going stun:
Dam, dab and dangerous to wonk.
You realise this ward you've led me into
Spelled backwards is the cloudy draw
Of the ghost-riders in the sky?
Listen to this palindrome
And tell me that it's not my ticket out.
Able was I ere I saw Elba.
Do you know who I am, Dr Larue?

Bigger than a Man

Bigger than a man, the wedding tackle
Of the male blue whale is a reminder
There can be potent spouses who stay true.

As he nuzzles up behind her
He gives hard evidence that he is always keen,
And when they have lain face to face awhile

Like two blimps that have seen *The Blue Lagoon*,
He brings the Sunday papers up to bed.
With a whole globe of ocean for a boudoir

Their pillow talk has not been much recorded,
But there have been some transcripts:
'Baweeng bok eeng,' he sings, and she:

'Baweeng chock. Eeng bawok eeng chunk.'
Some experts think that 'eeng' must mean 'again':
She asks for more of what he always gives.

Well, that would fit, as his impressive member
Lodges in her blancmange-lined sleeping bag.
There are no blue whale marriage guidance counsellors

Except perhaps one, seen alone near Cape Town.
She sang 'eeng', always with a plangent cadence.
She sang 'eeng' only. 'Eeng eeng. Eeng eeng eeng.'

Publisher's Party

(for Posy Simmonds)

Young ladies beautiful as novelists
Were handing out the nibbles and the drinks.
Butch writers with bald heads and hairy wrists
Exchanged raised eyebrows, nudges, knowing winks,
Hints broader than their beams.
The tall dark knockout who prowled like a lynx
With the chicken satay cooled the optimists –
Her polite smile said *as if* and *in your dreams.*

One writer never sought her violet eyes.
He concentrated on the parquet floor.
Ungainly yet of no impressive size,
Lacking in social skills, licensed to bore,
He was the kind of bloke
A girl like her would normally ignore,
Unless, of course, he'd won the Booker Prize.
Alas, he had. I can't think of a joke –

Only of how she lingered there until
He woke up to the full force of her looks;
Of how we rippled with a jealous thrill,
All those of us who'd also written books
Out of an inner need;
And now a panel-game of hacks and crooks
Had staked him out for her to stalk and kill –
As if the man could write, and she could read.

They live in Docklands now: a top-floor flat
They can see France from. Yes, they live there, too:
A house in the Dordogne. Stuff like that
I honestly don't care about, do you?
But then I see her face
Beside his in the papers. Strange, but true –
Blind chance that picked his fame out of a hat
Had perfect vision when it gave him grace.

My new book's hopeless and I'm getting fat.

Literary Lunch

Reciting poetry by those you prize –
Auden, MacNeice, Yeats, Stevens, Charlotte Mew –
I trust my memory and watch your eyes
To see if you know I am wooing you
With all these stolen goods. Of course you do.

Across the table, you know every line
Does service for a kiss or a caress.
Words taken out of other mouths, in mine
Are a laying on of hands in formal dress,
And your awareness measures my success

While marking out its limits. You may smile
For pleasure, confident my love is pure:
What would have been an exercise in guile
When I was young and strong, is now for sure
Raised safely to the plane of literature,

Where you may take it as a compliment
Unmixed with any claims to more delight
Than your attention. Such was my intent
This morning, as I planned what to recite
Just so you might remember me tonight,

When you are with the man who has no need
Of any words but his, or even those:
The only poem that he cares to read
Is open there before him. How it flows
He feels, and how it starts and ends he knows.

At School with Reg Gasnier

Gasnier had soft hands that the ball stuck to
And a body swerve off either foot
That just happened, you couldn't see him think.
He wasn't really knock-kneed
But he looked that way when he ran,
With his studded ankles flailing sideways
Like the hubcaps of a war chariot.
At tackling practice we went at him in despair
And either missed or fell stunned,
Our foreheads dotted with bleeding sprig-marks.
So glorious were his deeds
That the testimonials at school assembly
On the day after the match
Went on like passages from Homer.
He put Sydney Tech on the football map.
There were whole GPS teams he went through
Like a bat through a dark cave.
Sydney High, with backs the size of forwards,
Only barely stopped him,
And they practically used land mines.
Wanting to be him, I so conspicuously wasn't
That I would brood for hours in the library,
One kid from Kogarah utterly wiped out
By the lustre of another.
Later on, as a pro, he won national fame.
His shining story followed me to England:
I couldn't get away from the bastard.
By the time I got a slice of fame myself –
And we're talking about the echo of a whisper –
His nephew Mark was playing:

Clear proof that the gift was in the blood.
Reg is retired now
And not writing as many poems as I am,
But give me my life again and I would still rather
Be worshipped in the school playground
By those who saw him score the winning try,
A human dodgem snaking through a bunch of blokes
All flying the wrong way like literary critics –
Or at least I think so,
Now that I can't sleep without socks on.

At Ian Hamilton's Funeral

Another black tie invitation comes:
And once again, the black tie is the long
Thin one and not the bow. No muffled drums
Or stuff like that, but still it would be wrong
To flout the solemn forms. Fingers and thumbs
Adjust the knot as I recall the song
About the gang that sang 'Heart of My Heart'.
Death brings together what time pulled apart.

In Wimbledon, a cold bright New Year's Eve
Shines on the faces that you used to know
But only lights the depth to which they grieve
Or are beginning to. The body-blow
You dealt us when you left we will believe
When it sinks in. We haven't let you go
As yet. Outside the church, you're here with us.
Whatever's said, it's you that we discuss.

We speak of other things, but what we mean
Is you, and who you were, not where you are.
No one would call the centre of the scene
That little box inside the big black car.
Two things we wish were true: you made a clean
Getaway, and you have not gone far.
One thing we're sure of: now the breath is fled
You aren't in there, you're somewhere else instead –

Safe in a general memory. We file
Inside. The London literati take
Their places pew to pew and aisle to aisle
At murmured random. Nothing is at stake

Except the recollection of your smile.
All earned it. Who most often? For your sake
Men wrote all night, and as for women, well,
How many of them loved you none can tell.

Those who are here among us wear the years
With ease, as fine-boned beauty tends to do.
It wasn't just your looks that won the tears
They spill today when they remember you.
Most of us had our minds on our careers.
You were our conscience, and your women knew
Just by our deference the man in black
Who said least was the leader of the pack.

Dressed all your life for mourning, you made no
Display. Although your prose was eloquent,
Your poetry fought shy of outward show.
Pain and regret said no more than they meant.
Love sued for peace but had nowhere to go.
Joy was a book advance already spent,
And yet by day, free from the soul's midnight,
Your conversation was a sheer delight.

Thirsty for more of it, we came to drink
In Soho. While you read his manuscript
You gave its perpetrator time to think
Of taking up another trade. White-lipped
He watched you sneer. But sometimes you would blink
Or nod or even chuckle while you sipped
Your scotch, and then came the acceptance fee:
The wit, the gossip, the hilarity.

You paid us from your only source of wealth.
Your finances were always in a mess.

We told each other we did good by stealth.
In private we took pride in a success:
Knowing the way of life that wrecked your health
Was death-defying faith, not fecklessness,
We preened to feel your hard-won lack of guile
Rub off on us for just a little while.

For lyric truth, such suffering is the cost –
So the equation goes you incarnated.
The rest of us must ponder what we lost
When we so prudently equivocated.
But you yourself had time for Robert Frost –
His folksy pomp and circumstance you hated,
Yet loved his moments of that pure expression
You made your own sole aim if not obsession.

Our quarrel about that's not over yet,
But here today we have to let it rest.
The disagreements we could not forget
In life, will fade now and it's for the best.
Your work was a sad trumpet at sunset.
My sideshow razzmatazz you rarely blessed
Except with the reluctant grin I treasured
The most of all the ways my stuff was measured.

Laughter in life, and dark, unsmiling art:
There lay, or seemed to lie, the paradox.
Which was the spirit, which the mortal part?
As if in answer, borne aloft, the box
Goes by one slow step at a time. The heart
At last heaves and the reservoir unlocks
Of sorrow. That was you, and you are gone:
First to the altar, then to oblivion.

The rest is ceremony, and well said.
Your brother speaks what you would blush to hear
Were you alive and standing with bowed head.
But you lie straight and hidden, very near
Yet just as far off as the other dead
Each of us knows will never reappear.
You were the governor, the chief, the squire,
And now what's left of you leaves for the fire.

Ashes will breed no phoenix, you were sure
Of that, but not right. You should hear your friends
Who rise to follow, and outside the door
Agree this is a sad day yet it ends
In something that was not so clear before:
The awareness of love, how it defends
Itself against forgetfulness, and gives
Through death the best assurance that it lives.

Press Release from Plato

Delayed until the sacred ship got back
From Delos, the last hour of Socrates
Unfolded smoothly. His time-honoured knack
For putting everybody at their ease

Was still there even while the numbness spread
Up from his feet. All present in the cell
Were much moved by the way he kept his head
As he spoke less, but never less than well.

Poor Crito and Apollodorus wept
Like Xanthippe, but not one tear was his
From start to finish. Dignity was kept.
If that much isn't certain, nothing is.

I only wish I could have been there too.
When, later on, I wrote down every word,
I double-checked – the least that I could do –
To make it sound as if I'd overheard.

But let's face facts. He lives because of me.
That simple-seeming man and what he meant
To politics and to philosophy –
These things have not survived by accident.

Deals to be done and details to discuss
Called me elsewhere. I'm sorry for that still.
He owed a cock to Aesculapius.
Socratic question: guess who paid the bill?

Young Lady Going to Dakar

Another annual boat trip from Le Havre
To Bordeaux, but this time different. When Lautrec
Beheld the girl from Cabin 54
On deck reading, he decided to stay on
Until Lisbon at least. Painting had raised
The Paris cabarets, dance-halls and brothels
To angelic levels, but this unclouded creature
Started where all that finished. How not dream –
As she in her deckchair read and he nearby
Sketched for *La Passagère du cinquante-quatre:*
Promenade en yacht – that she would see his tears
And ask him to come with her to Dakar,
There to return his looks with the same favour,
Even for his legs? The painter's friend
Maurice Gilbert howled down the mad idea
Of Africa. They got off at Lisbon
And returned to Bordeaux overland.
In Toledo, for the first time in his life,
He saw El Greco. Dry-eyed, he took on
More strength, as if more strength were what he needed,
And not what he would instantly have traded
For just one glance from her untouched by pity:
Not even playful. Casual would have done.
The naked flame behind that cabin door!
Perish the thought. Paint her and finish her,
Drowned like the Holy Name in molten gold.

Ramifications of Pure Beauty

Passing the line-up of the narrow-boats
The swans proceed down river. As they go
They sometimes dip and lift an inch or so.
A swan is not a stick that merely floats
With the current. Currents might prove too slow
Or contrary. Therefore the feet deploy:
Trailed in the glide, they dig deep for the thrust
That makes the body bob. Though we don't see
The leg swing forward and extend, it must
Do so. Such a deduction can't destroy
Our sense-impression of serenity,
But does taint what we feel with what we know.

Bounced from up-sun by Focke-Wulf 'Long Nose'
Ta-152s, Pierre Clostermann
Noted their bodies 'fined down by the speed':
And so they were, to his eyes. Glider wings,
Long legs and close-cowled engine made the pose
Of that plane poised when stock-still. In the air,
High up and flat out, it looked fleet indeed.
What pulled it through the sky was left implied:
You had to know the turning blades were there,
Like the guns, the ammo and the man inside
Who might have thought your Tempest pretty too –
But not enough to stop him killing you.

The crowds for Titian cope with the appeal
Of flayed Actaeon. Horror made sublime:
We see that. Having seen it, we relax
With supine ladies. Pin-ups of their time,

Surely they have no hinterland of crime?
Corruption would show up like needle-tracks.
No, they are clean, as he was. All he knew
Of sin was painting them with not much on.
Even to fill a Spanish contract, he
Fleshed out the abstract with the sumptuous real –
Brought on the girls and called it poetry.
Philip II felt the same. Why think
At this late date about the mortal stink
Of the war galley, graceful as a swan?

The Serpent Beguiled Me

Following Eve, you look for apple cores
Along the riverbank, tossed in the mud.
Following Adam down long corridors,
You swing your torch to look for spit and blood.

He got his chest condition when he learned
Contentment made her curious. He thought
He was enough for her, and what he earned
Would keep her pinned while he played covert sport.

Alas, not so. She claimed that privilege too,
And even, under wraps, nursed the same pride
In taking satiation as her due –
A cue to call herself dissatisfied.

That rate of change was coded by the tree
Into the fruit. The instant thrill of sin
Turned sweet release to bitter urgency:
His fig leaf was flicked off, and hers sucked in.

From that day forth, the syrup she gave down
Smacked of the knowledge that she felt no shame.
The modesty for which she won renown
Was feigned to keep her freedom free of blame.

There was a time when, if he had not worn
Her out, she would have lain awake and wept.
Why was the truth, we ask, so slow to dawn?
He should have guessed it from how well she slept.

And when she turned to him, as she did still,
Though the old compulsion was no longer there,
The readiness with which she drank her fill
Told him in vain her fancy lay elsewhere.

He never faced the fact until she went.
He tracked her down and asked her what was wrong.
For once she said exactly what she meant:
'It was perfect. It just went on too long.'

State Funeral

In memory of Shirley Strickland de la Hunty

Famous for overcoming obstacles
She finally finds one that checks her flight.
Hit by the leading foot, a hurdle falls:
Except when, set in concrete, it sits tight.

Not that she hit too many. Most she cleared,
Her trailing leg laid effortlessly flat.
As in repose, at full tilt she appeared
Blessed with a supple grace. On top of that

She studied physics, took a good degree,
Had several languages to read and speak.
Alone, she wasn't short of company:
In company she shone. She was unique

Even among our girl Olympians
For bringing the mind's power and body's poise
To perfect balance. Ancient Greeks had plans
Along those lines, but strictly for the boys.

Her seven medals in three separate Games
Should have been eight, but she retired content.
In time she sold the lot to feed the flames
Of her concern for the Environment.

Civic responsibility: but one
Kind of pollution lay outside her scope
To counteract. The races she had run
Were won now by sad cyborgs fuelled with dope.

It started in the East. The State required
Results that only science could supply.
The female victims, suitably rewired
For victory, could do everything but fly.

And if some wept for how they changed, too bad.
The doctors did what they were ordered to
And told the chosen ones they should be glad:
Drink this, and it will make a man of you.

The plague spread to the West, where money talked.
Poor women, like poor men, had much to gain
Through muscle. The bad bottle was uncorked.
They plucked their chins and thought it worth the pain.

Perhaps it was, yet one glimpse of Flo-Jo
Coiled in her starting blocks told you the cost.
Transmuted to a charging buffalo,
She mourned with painted nails for what she'd lost.

But more was lost than that. The time had come
When no one could be trusted any more
Because to play it straight seemed simply dumb,
And who remembered how things were before?

Desire beats scruple into second place.
Gratification makes a fool of thrift.
The only rules are Rafferty's. The race
Is to the sly that once was to the swift.

A brighter future, back there in the past,
Flared for a moment but it flickered out.
It speaks, our flag that flutters at half mast,
Of final silence. Let it silence doubt:

When Shirley raced, the wings on her spiked shoes
Were merely mythical, like Mercury's.
She did it unassisted, win or lose.
The world she did it in died by degrees

While she looked on. Now she is spared the sight
At last. The bobby-dazzler won't be back,
Who ran for love and jumped for sheer delight
In a better life and on a different track –

We have too much if she is what we lack.

This Is No Drill

Out on my singing teacher's patio
While waiting for my lesson, I sat smoking,
And on the flag-stone about three feet from my chair
A scoop of bird shit suddenly appeared.
It looked like a nouvelle cuisine hors d'oeuvre,
A brown-green snail-pulp dollop on a bed
Of mascarpone hardening to meringue
As I watched, stupefied. I searched the sky
And there was nothing. Clean sweep. Been and gone.
So high up that it flies with the U-2s
And sees the Earth's curve, this bird calculates
Trajectories with so much to factor in –
Cloud density, speed, height, wind over target –
The wonder is it didn't miss by miles.
Instead, the point of impact was so close
The shock wave took the air out of my lungs.
Inside the house I croaked scales, and remembered
That day in the Piazza Santa Croce –
It must be thirty years back, maybe more –
When I got taken out by such a load
I felt the weight, and had to sit around
While the gunk dried on my brand new jacket. Why
These sneak attacks? We give them enough aid.
At least Prometheus and Tippi Hedren
Could see them coming. This is something else.
What do they want, a seat at the UN?
And no use asking if I would have died
Had this one nailed me. When a man is bald
And soon to face an aria from *Tosca*,
It's not as if he needs a pile of crap

Dumped on his head from fifty thousand feet
By some Stealth fowl. And spare me the assurance
That it wipes off. I didn't sign on for this.

Tramps and Bowlers

In the park in front of my place, every night
A bunch of tramps sleep on the wooden porch
Of the bowling green club-house. They shed no light.
No policeman ever wakes them with a torch,

Because no one reports their nightly stay.
People like me who take an early walk
Just after dawn will see them start the day
By packing up. They barely even talk,

Loading their duffel bags. They leave no trace,
Thus proving some who sleep rough aren't so dumb.
Tramps blow their secret if they trash the place:
This lot make sure that, when the bowlers come,

There's not a beer-can to pollute the scene.
And so, by day, neat paragons of thrift
And duty bow down to the very green
Which forms, by night, for scruffs who merely drift,

Their front lawn. If the bowlers only knew,
For sure they'd put in for a higher fence.
They'd have a point, but it would spoil the view
More than the tramps will, if they have the sense

To keep on cleaning up before they go,
Protecting indolence with industry:
A touch of what the bowlers value so.
Which way of life is better? Don't ask me –
I chose both, so I'd be the last to know.

Fires Burning, Fires Burning

Over Hamburg
The Lancaster crews could feel the heat
Through the sides of the aircraft.
The fire was six thousand feet high.

At Birkenau
When burning a lot of bodies, the SS found
The thing to do was to put down a layer
Of women first.
They had more fat in them.

In Tokyo
Some people who survived in a canal
Saw a horse on fire running through the streets.
But few who saw it were left to remember anything:
Even the water burned.

In New York
Some couples, given the choice
Between the flames and a long fall,
Outflanked the heat and went down holding hands.
Come with me, you imagine the men saying,
I know a quicker way.

In Sydney
Next to my mother's coffin
I gave thanks that she would shortly meet
A different kind of fire,
Having died first, and in due time.

Yusra

The Public Morals Unit of Hamas
Saw Yusra al-Azzuri, bold as brass,
In Gaza City, walk with her betrothed,
Her sister also present. Half unclothed,

All three behaved as if beyond the reach
Of justice. Laughing, dancing on the beach,
They almost touched. They thought to drive away.
The Unit followed them without delay.

Her young man drove. Beside him as they fled,
Yusra died quickly in a hail of lead.
The other two were hauled out of the car
And beaten senseless. With an iron bar,

The riddled corpse of Yusra, as the worst
Offender, was assaulted till it burst.
She would have prayed for death. It can be said,
Therefore, it was a blessing she was dead

Already. Thus we look for just one touch
Of grace in this catastrophe. Too much
To bear, the thought that those young men were glad
To be there. Won't the memory drive them mad?

Could they not see the laughter in her face
Was heaven on earth, the only holy place?
Perhaps they guessed, and acted from the fear
That Paradise is nowhere if not here.

Yusra, your name too lovely to forget
Shines like a sunrise joined to a sunset.
The day between went with you. Where you are,
That light around you is your life, Yusra.

Private Prayer at Yasukuni Shrine

An *Oka* kamikaze rocket bomb
Sits in the vestibule, its rising sun
Ablaze with pride.
Names of the fallen are on CD-ROM.
The war might have been lost. The peace was won:
A resurrection after suicide.

For once I feel the urge to send my thoughts
Your way, as I suppose these people do.
I see the tide
Come in on Papua. Their troop transports,
The beach, our hospital. Over to you:
Why was one little miracle denied?

After they made our nurses wade waist deep
They picked their targets and they shot them all.
The waves ran red.
Somehow this is a memory I keep.
I hear the lost cries of the last to fall
As if I, too, had been among the dead.

Those same troops fought south to the Golden Stairs,
Where they were stopped. They starved, and finally
The last few fed
On corpses. And the victory would be theirs
If I were glad? That's what you're telling me?
It would have been in vain that your son bled?

But wasn't it? What were you thinking when
Our daughters died? You couldn't interfere,
I hear you say.
That must mean that you never can. Well, then,
At least I know now that no prayers from here
Have ever made much difference either way,

And therefore we weren't fighting you as well.
Old people here saw the *Missouri* loom
Out in the bay
And thought the end had come. They couldn't tell
That the alternative to certain doom
Would be *pachinko* and the cash to play

A game of chance, all day and every day.
In that bright shrine you really do preside.
What you have said
Comes true. The DOW is down on the Nikkei.
The royal baby takes a buggy ride.
The last war criminal will die in bed.

Naomi from Namibia

In the Brisbane Botanical Gardens,
Walking the avenue of weeping figs,
You can see exuded latex stain the bark
Like adolescent sperm. A metamorphosis:
The trunks must be full of randy boys.

At home, the Java willows
When planted alongside a watercourse
Were said to stem the breeding of mosquitoes.
Here, they have nothing else to do
Except to stand there looking elegant
In Elle McPherson lingerie.

From the walkway through the mangrove mud-flats
Spread south from overwhelming Asia,
You can see the breathing tubes of Viet Cong crabs
And imagine Arnie hiding from the Predator
Like a mud-skipper playing possum,
Although he did that, of course, in South America.
Below the tangled branches, bubbles tick.

For a century and a half, the giant banyan
Has grown like a cathedral heading downwards,
As a dumb Chartres might slowly dive for cover
Through shallows clear as air. In India
At least a dozen families would be dying
By inches in its colonnades.

At the kiosk, Naomi from Namibia
Serves me a skimmed milk strawberry milkshake.
She has come here to lead her ideal life,
Like almost all these trees.
They get to stay, but she has to go back.

William Dobell's Cypriot

The Cypriot brought his wine-dark eyes with him
Along with his skin and hair. He also brought
That shirt. Swathes of fine fabric clothe a slim
Frame with a grace bespeaking taste and thought.

Australia, 1940. There were few
Men native-born who had that kind of style.
Hence the attention Dobell gave the blue
Collar and cuffs, to make us pause awhile

And see a presence that did not belong.
This sitter, sitting here, caught by this hand?
Caught beautifully. No, there is nothing wrong
About this transportation to Queensland

Of ancient subtleties. It's merely odd.
A man whom he had loved and seen asleep
The painter painted naked, a Greek god.
But then he had the sudden wit to keep

The clothes, and thus the heritage, in the next
Picture. A window from a men's-wear store,
It doubles as the greatest early text
Of the immigration. What we were before

Looks back through this to what we would become.
We see a sense of nuance head our way
To make the raw rich, complicate the sum
Of qualities, prepare us for today.

Now that the day is ours, the time arrives
To remember destiny began as chance,
And history is as frail as human lives.
A young and foreign smile, love at first glance:

Painter and painted possibly first met
Just because one admired the other's tie.
A year old then, I live now in their debt.
This is the way they live. I too will die.

Ghost Train to Australia

(Container Train in Landscape, 1983–84, by Jeffrey Smart)

I won't this time. Silent at last and shunted
Into its siding in the Victorian Arts Centre,
The container train started its journey in Yugoslavia
Two years before it arrived in Gippsland
Among trees that echo Albert Namatjira.

The containers echo First World War dazzle paint
Whose solid planes of colour fooled submarines.
Everything in the picture echoes something,
Yet it all belongs to the painter's unifying vision.
How does he do that? Perhaps as a consolation

For not being Piero della Francesca
And lacking Christ's birth to celebrate in Arezzo,
He can alter the order of modern history's pages
Though we might need our memories to catch him in
         the act:
All trains in Europe, for example, even today,

When they are drawn by electric locos and made of metal,
Remind us of boxcars full of unbelieving people
And the scenes on the platform when the train pulled in.
No amount of lusciously applied colour
Can cover all that stark grey squalor up

Or take away the shadow on a train's fate.
Simply because it is a European train,
Even if it goes all the way to Australia
And terminates among the eucalypts
In a lake of perfect sunlight the whole sky deep

And everybody gets off and there are no searchlights
Or whips or wolf-hounds or cold-eyed efficient doctors
And the fathers go to work on the Snowy River
And the mothers learn the lemon meringue pie
And the children, after they have had their tonsils out,

Get Shelley's lemonade and vanilla ice-cream
And all grow up to be captain of the school,
And the local intellectuals fly in like fruit-bats
To lecture the new arrivals about genocide,
The train, the train, the wonderful train

That found visas for all aboard and now finally sits
Shining in the bush like five bob's worth of sweets –
Jaffas, Cherry Ripes, Hoadley's Violet Crumble Bars
Glittering in the original purple and gold wrappers –
Is still the ghost train. I'm sorry, I didn't mean to.

Les Saw It First

I swam across the creek at Inverell.
The guard of jacarandas bled their blue
Into the water. I recall it well,
But partly I do that because of you.

I was a city boy. A country trip
Was rare, and so the memories were sparse.
I helped to plait a cracker for a whip,
But when I swung the thing it was a farce.

At Tingha, where they used to mine the tin,
I searched for sapphires all day and found none.
I briefly rode a horse and barked my shin
When I got off, and couldn't stand the sun

That bleached the fence-rails to a dry, pale grey
A hundred years before and there they were,
Just looking wooden and what can you say?
Sit on a stump and blink into the blur.

I had been long away when I looked back
Through your books and at last saw what I'd seen:
The blue-tongue in the gum beside the track,
The headless black snake limp as Plasticine.

The snake was in a trench they called a race.
Somebody threw it there when it was dead.
Now I remember how fear froze my face
When, further on, I found its yawning head.

The country built the city: now I know.
Like it or not, it got to even me,
And not just through the Royal Easter Show,
But the hard yakka of its poetry.

Now I can hear the shouts of the young men
Out after rabbits with a .22.
I wasn't there long, but I'm there again,
Collecting trinkets as the magpies do.

It's part of me, and partly because of you.

Signed by the Artist

The way the bamboo leans out of the frame,
Some of its leaves cut short by the frame's edge,
Makes room for swathes of air which you would think,
If it were sold in bolts, would drape like silk.
Below, where one pond spills from the stone ledge
Into the next, three carp as white as milk
Glow through the water near the painter's name,
A stack of characters brushed in black ink.

The open spaces and the spare detail
Are both compressed into that signature:
He made his name part of the work of art.
Slice of crisp leaf, smooth flourish of fish fin
Are there to show you he is very sure
Of how the balance of things kept apart
Can shape a distance. On a larger scale
He still leaves out far more than he puts in.

We're lucky that he does. What he includes,
Almost too beautiful to contemplate,
Already hurts our hearts. Were he to fill
The gaps, the mind would have no place to rest,
No peace in the collected solitudes
Of those three fish, in how each leaf is blessed
With life. Easy to underestimate
A name like his. No substance. Too much skill.

Return of the Lost City

How far was Plato free of that 'inflamed
Community' he said we should avoid?
Sofas, incense and hookers: these he named
Among the habits not to be enjoyed,
And if you did, you ought to be ashamed.
But can't we tell, by how he sounds annoyed,
That his Republic, planned on our behalf,
Was where his own desires had the last laugh,

If only as the motor for his sense
Of discipline? Even the dreams were policed,
By the Nocturnal Council. Such immense
Powers of repression! What would be released
Without them? The Republic was intense:
The fear of relaxation never ceased.
Hence the embargo on all works of art,
However strict in form, that touched the heart.

No poetry. No poets! No, not one –
Not even Homer, if he were to be
Reborn – could be admitted, lest the sun
Set on the hard-won social harmony,
And that obscene night-life which had begun
In man's first effort at society,
Atlantis, should come flooding back, the way
The sea did, or so story-tellers say.

But Plato knew that they'd say anything:
For money or applause or just a share
Of an hetaera, they would dance and sing
And turn the whole deal into a nightmare.

The very prospect left him quivering
With anger. There is something like despair
Haunting the author of the ideal state,
A taunting voice he heard while working late:

Atlantis made you. It is what you know,
Deep down. Atlantis and its pleasures drive
Your thoughts. Atlantis never lets you go.
Atlantis is where you are most alive –
Yes, even you, you that despise it so,
When all mankind would love it to arrive
Again, the living dream you try to kill
By making perfect. But you never will.

Anniversary Serenade

You are my alcohol and nicotine,
My silver flask and cigarette machine.
You watch and scratch my back, you scrub me clean.
I mumble but you still know what I mean.
Know what I mean?
You read my thoughts, you see what I have seen.

You are my egg-flip and my ego trip,
My passion-fruit soufflé and strawberry whip.
When the dawn comes to catch you on the hip
I taste the sweet light on my fingertip.
My fingertip?
I lift it to my quivering lips and sip.

Homecoming Queen and mother of our two
Smart daughters who, thank God, take after you,
This house depends on what you say and do –
And all you do is wise and say is true.
And say is true?
True as a plumb-line or a billiard cue.

On from Byzantium to Cooch Behar
Our Messerschmitt two-seater bubble car,
Laden with foie gras and with caviare,
Follows the shining road to Shangri-la.
To Shangri-la?
With Blossom Dearie singing in the bar.

When the sun fades, the Earth will fly away.
Tell me it isn't happening today.
I have a debt of happiness to pay.

I die if you should leave, live if you stay.
Live if you stay?
Live like a king, proud as a bird of prey.

My share of Heaven and my sheer delight,
My soda fountain and my water-sprite,
My curving ribbon of a climbing kite,
You are my Starlight Roof, my summer night.
My summer night?
The flying foxes glide, the possums fight.

You are my honeydew and panther sweat,
The music library on my private jet.
Top of the bill, we fly without a net.
You are the stroke of luck I can't forget.
I can't forget?
I'm still not ready for you even yet.

You are my nicotine and alcohol,
My Stéphane Audran in a Claude Chabrol,
My sunlight through a paper parasol,
My live-in living doll and gangster's moll –
And gangster's moll?
Mine the fedora, yours the folderol.

The ring is closed. The rolling dice we cast
So long ago still roll but not so fast.
The colours fade that we nailed to the mast
We lose the future but we own the past.
We own the past?
From our first kiss, a lifetime to the last.

Double or Quits

Sydney, 2006

Only when we are under different skies
The truth strikes home of what love has become:
A compact it takes time to realise
Is better far, being less burdensome,
Than that first tempest by which we were torn.
Tonight you're there, where both of us now live,
And I am here, where both of us were born,
But there is no division we need give
A thought to, beyond localised regret:
For we will be together again soon,
And both see the one sunrise and sunset
And the face saved and the face lost by the moon –
The clouds permitting, which they seldom do
In England, but at least I'll be with you.

I'll be with you from now on to the end
If you say so. Should you choose otherwise
Then I will be a jealous loving friend
To wish you well yet prove it never dies,
Desire. Your beauty still bewilders me
Though half a century has passed. I still
Stand breathless at the grace of what I see:
More so than ever, now the dead leaves fill
The garden. A long distance will soon come.
Today, no. Nor tomorrow. But it must
Open the door into Elysium
For one of us, and me the first, I trust.
May we stay joined, as these two sonnets are –
That meet, and are apart, but just so far.

Overview

An object lesson in the speed of silence,
The condensation trail across the sky
High over London scores the Wedgwood blue
With one long streak of chalk so true and pure
It seems an angel has begun to crop-dust
The lower fields of Heaven.

Nothing is where you think it is for long.
Our granddaughter, here for a Sunday visit,
Goes through the house like a burst of friendly fire
Or a cosmic particle making its instant transit
Of a bubble chamber. A close search of my corpse
Would find the trajectory of her smile.

Convinced all lasting memories are digital,
The clump of Japanese tourists at Tower Bridge
Hold up their telephones like open notebooks.
As part of their plan, surely now near completion,
For copying the Earth,
They snap the coke-line in the stratosphere.

Our granddaughter would not sit still for that.
My wife gets pictures only of where she was.
Our elder daughter says the thing observed
Changes the observer: it works both ways.
Our younger daughter is reading *Mansfield Park*,
But the cat yawns the soft first syllable

Of Schrödinger's name. Everything happens now.
None of it hangs together except in thought,
And that, too, will pass. One ought to take
Solace from the resplendent, but it goes hard
To know the world view that you had in mind
Is fading like powdered water,
Your mark lost in the thin air it was made from.

The Nymph Calypso

Planning to leave Calypso in the lurch,
Odysseus snuck off to build a ship.
He found the right-shaped boughs of larch or birch
Or spruce, for all I know, from which to strip
The bark, and . . . but the details we can skip.
I won't pretend that I've done much research.
He had to build a ship and he knew how.
Just how he did it hardly matters now:

Enough to say he juggled rib and spar.
Calypso came to him and said, 'I see
That duty calls. Will you be going far?
You wouldn't have your mind on leaving me,
By any chance? Forget the trickery
For once, and if you're following your star
Just say so. Circe lured you with a song.
At least I wasn't stringing you along.'

'It's time,' he said. 'I'm an adventurer.
I sail in search of things. It's what I do.
I'd heard about how beautiful you were,
So lovely that I came in search of you.
But now I know you and need something new
To challenge me.' He wryly smiled at her
To show he knew he sounded like a ham.
'You wanted me. Well, this is what I am.'

'All very well,' Calypso said, 'but I
Have an investment here. You had to quit

Sometime, and I gave you a reason why.
Old studs like you need youth to love. I'm it.
I'm always eager, and you're still quite fit:
A last adventure to light up the sky.
I'll tell my tale forever, don't forget:
The greatest lover that I ever met.'

Odysseus could see the point, but still
He stood his ground, a man of destiny
Proclaiming his ungovernable will
To follow the unknown out to the sea
Beyond the sea, and solve the mystery
Of where the world went next, and not until
He had would he find rest. Calypso said,
'No wonder that you turned up here half dead.'

That night the two of them made love again.
She slapped herself against him when she came
The way she always did, but even then
She let him know she knew things weren't the same.
She cried out his polysyllabic name –
Something she'd never done for other men –
As if, this time, he was no longer there.
But though she flattered him with her despair,

Already he had made the break. His mind
Was elsewhere, on a course she could not guess.
She thought her hero had new worlds to find
Out on the edge of the blue wilderness,
But he had lied, to cause her less distress.
We needn't think of him as being kind:
He simply knew the truth would drive her mad
And make her fight with everything she had.

After he left, she let the world believe
She'd given him the boat: a likely tale
That Homer swallowed whole. Keen to deceive
Even herself, for no nymph likes to fail –
The Miss World of the Early Age of Sail
Had never yet known such a cause to grieve –
She spread the story that he'd only gone
Because she told him legends must go on.

But he was going home. There, in the end,
Lay the departure point for his last quest.
Age was a wound that time indeed would mend
But only one way, with a long, long rest.
For that, familiar territory is best.
As for Penelope, he could depend
On her care for the time he had to live.
Calypso wanted more than he could give,

And it was time to take, time to accept
The quiet bounty of domestic peace.
After he killed the suitors who had kept
His wife glued to the loom, she spread the fleece
Of their first blanket and they found release
Together as they once had. Though she wept
For their lost years, she gave him her embrace,
And he looked down into her ageing face

And saw Calypso. What the nymph would be,
Given the gift of time, was there made plain,
Yet still more beautiful. Penelope,
Because she knew that we grow old in pain
And learn to laugh or else we go insane,
Had life unknown to immortality,

Which never gets the point. 'Well, quite the boy,'
She murmured. 'And now tell me about Troy.'

Later the poets said he met his fate
In the Atlantic, or perhaps he went
Around the Horn and reached the Golden Gate.
Space vehicles named after him were sent
Into infinity. His testament,
However, and what truly made him great,
Was in the untold story of the day
He died, and, more or less, had this to say:

'Penelope, in case you ever hear
The nymph Calypso loved me, it was so:
And she tried everything to keep me near
But finally she had to let me go
Because she knew I loved you. Now you know,
And I can move on, having made that clear.'
And so he did, while she knelt by his side,
Not knowing, as he sailed on the last tide,

That just this once he almost hadn't lied.

Meteor IV at Cowes, 1913

Sydney in spring. Tonight you dine alone.
Walk up the Argyle Cut to Argyle Place
And turn left at the end. In there you'll find
Fish at the Rocks: not just a fish-and-chip joint
But a serious restaurant, with tablecloths
And proper glassware. On the walls, a row
Of photographs, all bought as a job lot
By a decorator with a thoughtful eye:
Big portraits of the racing yachts at Cowes
In the last years before the First World War.
Lustrous in black and white as deep as sepia,
The photographs are framed in the house style
Of Beken, the smart firm that held the franchise
And must have had a fast boat of its own
To catch those vivid poses out at sea:
Swell heaving in the foreground, sky for backdrop,
Crew lying back on tilting teak or hauling
On white sheets like the stage-hands of a classic
Rope-house theatre shifting brilliant scenery –
Fresh snowfields, arctic cliffs, wash-day of titans.
What stuns you now is the aesthetic yield:
A mere game made completely beautiful
By time, the winnower, whose memory
Has taken out all but the lasting outline,
The telling detail, the essential shadow.
But nothing beats the lovely, schooner-rigged
Meteor IV, so perfectly proportioned
She doesn't show her size until you count
The human hieroglyphs carved on her deck
As she heels over. Twenty-six young men

Are present and correct below her towers
Of canvas. At the topmost point, the apex
Of what was once a noble way of life
Unquestioned as the antlers in the hunting lodge,
The Habsburg eagle flies. They let her run,
Led by the foresail tight as a balloon,
Full clip across the wind, under the silver sun,
Believing they can feel this thrill for ever –
And death, though it must come, will not come soon.

The Magic Wheel

An ode in the manner of Theocritus

O magic wheel, draw hither to my house the man I love.
I dreamed of you as dreaming that, and now
The boxed-in balcony of my hotel room high above
Grand Harbour is a sauna. See the prow
Of that small boat cut silk. Out in the sea
No waves, and there below not even ripples turning light
To glitter: just a glow spread evenly
On flawless water spills into the skyline that last night
Was a jewelled silhouette from right to left and left to right.

Behold, the sea is silent, and silent are the winds.
The not yet risen sun edges the sky
With petal-juice of the Homeric rose as day begins.
I am alone, but with you till I die,
Now we have met again after six years.
Last night we danced on limestone in the open-air café.
I saw one woman sitting there near tears,
Aware that she would never look like you or dance that way –
A blessing, like the blessings that have brought you home to stay.

O magic wheel, draw hither to my house the man I love.
I dreamed of you as dreaming that, until
I saw you wave in welcome from your window high above,
And up the slick hard steps designed to kill,
Like all Valletta staircases bar none,
I went, as if I still had strength, to find your open door
And you, and your tremendous little son,

And your husband, the great dancer, whom I had not met before,
And I met his kindly eyes and knew you dreamed of me no more.

Behold, the sea is silent, and silent are the winds.
Stirred by the ceiling fan, the heat of noon
Refuses to grow cooler as it very slowly spins,
But I take its rearrangement as a boon,
As if it were the gradual work of time,
Which leaves things as they are but changes us and picks the hour
To make us see resentment is a crime.
A loving memory forgets and true regret yields power:
Trust in the long slow aqueduct and not the water tower.

O magic wheel, draw hither to my house the man I love.
I dreamed of you as dreaming that. Tonight
My dream was gone, but flowering in the darkness high above
The *festa*, rockets set the rain alight,
The soft, sweet rain. With you and your young men,
I walked the shining streets and all was right and nothing wrong
As the joy of our first moment lived again.
In the ruins of the opera house a lizard one inch long
Is the small but vibrant echo of an interrupted song.

Bethink thee of my love and whence it comes, O holy Moon.
I dreamed of you as dreaming that, and now
I know you never did. Another day: the afternoon
Burns white as only here the sun knows how,
But a fever is broken when I sweat –
For my delight in your contentment proves that in the past
My love must have been true, as it is yet:
The magic wheel has turned to show what fades and what holds fast.
Dream this when I am gone: that he was glad for me at last.

Portrait of Man Writing

While you paint me, I marvel at your skin.
The miracle of being twenty-four
Is there like a first blush as you touch in
The blemishes that make my face a war
I'm losing against time. So you begin,
By lending inwardness to an outline,
Your life in art as I am ending mine.

Try not to miss the story my mouth tells,
Even unmoving, of how once I had
The knack for capering in cap and bells,
And had to make an effort to seem sad.
These eyes that look as crusty as dry wells
Despite the glue they seep, once keenly shone.
Give them at least a glimmer of what's gone.

I know these silent prayers fall on deaf ears:
You've got integrity like a disease.
Bound to record the damage of the years,
You aim to tell the truth, and not to please.
And so this other man slowly appears
Who is not me as I would wish to be,
But is the me that I try not to see.

Suppose while you paint me I wrote of you
With the same fidelity: people would say
That not a line could possibly be true.
Nobody's lips in real life glow that way.
Silk eyelashes! Is this what he's come to?
Your portrait, put in words, sounds like a lie,
Minus the facts a glance would verify.

But do we credit beauty even when
It's there in front of us? It stops the heart.
The mortal clockwork has to start again,
Ticking towards the day we fall apart,
Before we see now all we won't have then.
Let's break for lunch. What progress have we made?
Ah yes. That's me exactly, I'm afraid.

Status Quo Vadis

As any good poem is always ending,
The fence looks best when it first needs mending.
Weathered, it hints it will fall to pieces –
One day, not yet, but the chance increases
With each nail rusting and grey plank bending.
It's not a wonder if it never ceases.

In beauty's bloom you can see time burning:
A lesson learned while your guts are churning.
Her soft, sweet cheek shows the clear blood flowing
Towards the day when her looks are going
Solely to prove there is no returning
The way they came. There's a trade wind blowing.

We know all this yet we love forever.
Build her a fence and she'll think you're clever.
Write her a poem that's just beginning
From start to finish. You'll wind up winning
Her heart, perhaps, but be sure you'll never
Hold on to the rainbow the top sets spinning.

What top? The tin one that starts to shiver
Already, and soon will clatter. The river
Of colour dries up and your mother's calling
Your name while the ball hasn't finished falling,
And you miss the catch and you don't forgive her.
You went out smiling but you go home bawling.

Weep all you like. Earn your bread from weeping.
Write reams explaining there is no keeping
The toys on loan, and proclaim their seeming
Eternal glory is just the dreaming
We do pretending that we aren't sleeping –
Your tears are stinging? They're diamonds gleaming.

Think of it that way and reap the splendour
That flares reflected in the chromium fender
Of the Chrysler parked in the concrete crescent.
The surge is endless, the sigh incessant.
A revelation can only tender
Sincere regrets from the evanescent.

Remember this when it floods your senses
With streams of light and the glare condenses
Into a star. It's a star that chills you.
Don't fool yourself that the blaze fulfils you
And builds your bridges and mends your fences
Merely because of the way it thrills you –

The breath of life is what finally kills you.

Dreams Before Sleeping

The idea is to set the mind adrift
And sleep comes. Mozart, exquisitely dressed,
Walks carefully to work between soft piles
Of fresh horse-dung. Nice work. Why was my gift
Hidden behind the tree? I cried for miles.
No one could find it. Find the tiger's face.
It's in the tree: i.e. the strangest place.

But gifts were presents then. In fact, for short,
We called them pressies, which was just as long,
But sounded better. Mallarmé thought 'night'
A stronger word than *nuit*. Nice word. The fort
Defied the tide but faded like a song
When the wave's edge embraced it at last light.
Which song? Time, time, it is the strangest thing.
The Waves. The Sea, the Sea. Awake and Sing.

Wrong emphasis, for music leads to sex.
Your young man must be stroking you awake
Somewhere about now, in another time.
Strange thing. Range Rover. Ducks de Luxe. *Lex rex.*
The cherry blossoms fall into the lake.
The carp cruise undisturbed. Lemon and lime
And bitters is a drink for drinkers. Just.
I who was iron burn in silence. Rust.

What would you do to please me, were you here?
The *tarte tatin* is melting the ice cream.
One sip would murder sleep, but so does this.
Left to itself, the raft floats nowhere near

Oblivion, or even a real dream.
Strange word, nice question. Real? Real as a kiss,
Which never lasts, but proves we didn't waste
The time we spent in longing for its taste.

Seek sleep and lose it. Fight it and it comes.
I knew that, but it's too late now. The bird
Sings with its wings. The turtle storms ashore.
Pigs fly. Would that translate to talking drums?
Nice if they didn't understand a word
Each other said, but drowned in metaphor –
As we do when we search within, and find
Mere traces of the peace we had in mind.

Forget about it. Just get up and write.
But when you try to catch that cavalcade,
Too much coherence muscles in. Nice thought.
Let's hear it, heartbreak. Happiness writes white.
Be grateful for the bed of nails you made
And now must lie in, trading, as you ought,
Sleep for the pictures that will leave you keen
To draft a memo about what they mean.

You will grow weary doing so. Your eyes
Are fighting to stay open. When they fail
You barely make it back to where you lay.
What do you see? Little to memorize.
A lawn shines green again through melting hail.
Deep in its tree, a tiger turns away.
Nice try, but it was doomed, that strange request
To gaze into the furnace and find rest.

The Carnival

You can't persuade the carnival to stay.
Wish all you like, it has to go away.
Don't let the way it moves on get you down.
If it stayed put, how could it come to town?

How could there be the oompah and the thump
Of drums, the trick dogs barking as they jump?
The girl in pink tights and gold headache-band
Still smiling upside down in a hand stand?

These wonders get familiar by the last
Night of the run. A miracle fades fast.
You spot the pulled thread on a leotard.
Those double somersaults don't look so hard.

Can't you maintain your childish hunger? No.
They know that in advance. They have to go,
Not to return until they're something new
For anybody less blasé than you.

The carnival, the carnival. You grieve,
Knowing the day must come when it will leave.
But that was why her silver slippers shone –
Because the carnival would soon be gone.

We Being Ghosts

Too many of my friends are dead, and others wrecked
By various diseases of the intellect
Or failing body. How am I still upright?
And even I sleep half the day, cough half the night.

How did it come to this? How else but through
The course of years, and what its workings do
To wood, stone, glass and almost all the metals,
Smouldering already in the fresh rose petals.

Our energy deceived us. Blessed with the knack
To get things done, we thought to get it back
Each time we lost it, just by taking breath –
And some of us are racing yet as we face death.

Well, good to see you. Sorry I have to fly.
I'm struggling with a deadline, God knows why,
And ghosts keep interrupting. Think of me
The way I do of you. Quite often. Constantly.